Heartbreak Autopsy

poems by
Amanda McLeod

Advance Praise for *Heartbreak Autopsy*

"*Heartbreak Autopsy* shimmers with heat and hurt, damage and disillusionment. McLeod writes fearless poetry which is sometimes startling, often beautiful, and always straight-talking. These poems are unsentimental, poignant and raw, demonstrating a deep understanding of the vagaries of the human heart."

—Amanda Huggins, author of *The Collective Nouns for Birds* and *All Our Squandered Beauty*

"'Putting on protective gear means admitting you know what you're about to do could hurt you,' Amanda McLeod warns in *Heartbreak Autopsy*. Well, shrug into your hi-vis vest, strap on a helmet, and buckle up. This collection is a little bit anything-is-possible summer and a little bit tornado through your small town."

—Lannie Stabile, author of *Good Morning to Everyone Except Men Who Name Their Dogs Zeus*

"These poems are pearls—some cultured, others wild. At the heart of each sits life's grit; seeding specks of passion, fury, joy and pain, around which McLeod has fashioned something quite special."

—Benjamin Dodds, author of *Airplane Baby Banana Blanket*

"In Amanda McLeod's remarkable and devastating *Heartbreak Autopsy*, you may find yourself dropped into the middle of a storm—you've got the ruby slippers, but the winds refuse to subside. As a bearing element, it's perfection for what's to come. Then, assured that there is no eye—no I—only the collective grief of loving and losing in a whirlwind, the inundation gathers personal elements that manage to ring universal, Bob Seger and cold beers, Holly Golightly, a hula dancer on the dash of a '67 Chevy, baseball, and Ariadne. It is a journey that presents a uniquely compelling interrogation of how chiseling the 'self' from the extraneous elements of interconnection can be violent, but ultimately a defining process."

—Kari Flickinger, author of *The Gull and the Bell Tower*

Heartbreak Autopsy

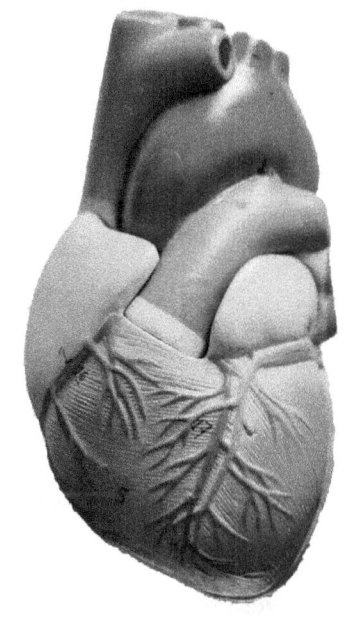

Amanda McLeod

Copyright © 2021 Amanda McLeod

All Rights Reserved. This book or any portion thereof may not be reproduced, in whole or in part, in any form (beyond that permitted by Sections 107 and 108 of the U.S Copyright Law and except by reviewers for the public press), without the express written permission of the publisher except for the use of brief quotations in a book review.

McLeod / Amanda, author

Heartbreak Autopsy / Amanda McLeod

Poems

ISBN: 978-1-7365167-4-4

Edited by: Beth Gordon
Book Design: Amanda McLeod
Cover Art: NeONBRAND via Unsplash
Cover Design: Amanda McLeod

PUBLISHER
Animal Heart Press
Thetford Center, Vermont 05075
www.animalheartpress.net

*for the lovers;
for the quiet griefs,
the mutual partings,
the sweet reliefs,
and all the other heartbreaks
that never made the front page.*

Table Of Contents

Storm Chasing	13
Heat	14
Mixed Grip	15
Reasons Not To Ride	16
The Water Diviner	17
Click My Heels	18
Crown: In Which The Mirror Tells The Truth	19
On Being Warded	21
Secrets	22
No Fury	23
Gunpowder Shimmer	24
In/Visible	25
Left Overs	26
Dealbreakers	27
Games People Play	28
Piano Bar, Just After 2am	29
It's Not Like That	30
Disassembly	31
There is Not Enough White in This Room	32
Le Langage de l'Amour	33
Aubade With Bus Stop	34
I want to write about change but the words won't come.	35
Self Possession	36
Return of Spontaneous Circulation	37

Acknowledgements *41*

About the Author *43*

Storm Chasing

The destruction is beautiful; from a distance she is
a shapely dancer trailing cloud-spiral scarves and swaying seduction but
proximity can be fatal. There are plenty of warning signs; a siren call,
a prickling of the hairs on the back of your neck, a breeze that picks up
and the sudden appearance of flying objects. A common error is the belief
that there is calm at the centre; for the briefest moment
you are lulled into complacency before the eye passes over you
and the wind now screams from the opposite direction.
Everything you thought was safe gets battered.
And yet, the damage is magnetic. You follow her,
awestruck by the trail in her wake, by the power
in her. To stand before her is to know all the fury
and passion of womanhood. Passion and power
are sexy. Anger beckons with honeyed
fingertips and you want to fall
on your knees and worship the
elemental energy pulsing from
her, even as she smashes glass
and brings others down with
her inner turbulence. What
would you give to understand
the bottomless well
of her strength?
To unravel her
secrets? Bring out
your instruments;
study her,
watch her intensify,
revel in her ferocity.
She is gravity, exploded atoms,
wind and fire.
And she will be
the end of you
if you stay
too
close.

Heat

Summer is a red and blue singlet
with a pair of jeans and a sliver of skin
suspended between them
like an invitation.
Bob Seger and cold beers on the couch
in the middle of the afternoon
like real life has been suspended
and responsibility melts like the asphalt outside.
Don't think about it. Let the heat haze settle
as the shadows lengthen. Your
problems will be waiting for you
when you get home, watching the clock,
wondering why you don't answer your phone
or the questions about where you've been.

Mixed Grip

I'm no closer to holding onto you
than I was the night you spun me
through the ocean waves and up
into the stars. Every shade of ink
gives way to rose and gold and
a faded version of itself. My skin
is the colour of water
and my breath is crystal,
untouchable but real
as any sunrise. Sweat lasts
longer on my skin than muscle
memory and cotton sticks to the slick
between my shoulders.
Gravity is the enemy
of movement. I hang, static, waiting
for the drop,
my chalked hands slipping, slipping--

Reasons Not To Ride

1. Putting on protective gear means admitting you know what you're about to do could hurt you.
2. There are one way signs on every block of what you know should be a two way street.
3. The road is riddled with hook turns; to go one way, you have to start going the other, and you never had a strong sense of direction.
4. When you're always riding pillion, you never get to steer.
5. You are the passenger; your safety depends on how tight you hold on. The driver never holds on to you.
6. You can break the speed limit but still be going round in circles.
7. The breathlessness of one wheel on the ground does not erase the danger of it.
8. Danger is seductive and adrenaline will keep pulling you back; one more time, one more time.
9. When you crash, you'll leave the scene and the haemothorax will suffocate you without anyone ever knowing the cause.

The Water Diviner

You'll be confident, at first. There are a thousand ways to find it. You'll wait on the reeded banks for something resembling a seasonal flow, but the stream tastes of silt and spiked cocktails. When it shrinks to puddles and eddied mud you'll shrug and take up your dowsing rod, certain you'll find a sweetwater spring or some other way to slake your thirst. But satisfaction will elude you; and you'll walk on through the strange familiar, laughing it off as the leaves shrivel and the ground becomes sand. Your smile will split your parched lips. You'll stumble on dew gathered in curled leaves, inviting in the predawn grey, but not enough to sustain you. Like salt, it will only increase your need. Your breath will become a desert wind, ragged in your throat. This pattern will continue, until the dry spell becomes a drought. And when it finally rains, you'll come so close to drowning you'll forget for a moment what it is to have oxygen in your lungs instead of water.

Click My Heels

I'm not in Kansas or anywhere else I recognise and strange mannequins with perfect hair take over street corners like riot police. The collar of my jacket isn't tall enough to keep my ears warm and the best coffee in the world is bitter on my tongue. I'd love to have breakfast at Tiffany's but it's not open and a small flashing light tells me where I'm not welcome. I'm the new Holly Golightly with a heavy step and unkempt hair; my mean reds are stormcloud grey, opaque. If I give *heartbreak* a name it'll stick around, so I'll make something up while I predict the weather for strangers and roam busy streets with an empty mind. If I click my heels three times I won't miss the plane and I can pretend the last three days in the right place with the wrong person were all just a dream.

Crown: In Which The Mirror Tells The Truth

This is not what either of us wanted;
your pursuit is relentless, but I am
afraid; the gilded cage feels too familiar.
My gentle explanation brings you no
solace; your white linen heart has fallen
hard. I wipe my grubby fingers and try
not to touch you. Keep my dirt to myself.
The river bank, broken like a promise,
crumbles underneath your confused footsteps.
Dreams wash away in the turgid current,
yours, and mine, and all I can do to stop
the pain is beg you to just let them go.
        I like you too much to hurt you like this;
        but I don't fit you and we both know it.

*

I'm a size too big, a poor fit, too loose
to cling to you and likely to fall down
without adjustment. If you tailor me to fit,
the parts you cut away will haunt us both—
I'll no longer be myself, and you'll be
left wondering what I might have been if
only you had kept me in one piece. A
gown, once altered, is never what it was.
Even when the fit is perfect, a good
tailor can see where it's been stitched back up;
what's gone is conspicuous by its absence.
Even healed wounds leave ghostly lines, scarring.
        It's not fair for us to cut ourselves up--
        neither one of us needs any more wounds.

*

We're wounded enough; everything you want
in your tomorrow is still far away
from mine, a shadow in a distant dawn.
Your closeness confuses me; I'm not sure
I deserve you, and you deserve better

than diamonds on a hesitant finger.
I'm not your stockhorse - the pressure of your
heel won't rein me in. Nor will your sweet words.
One of us must swallow disappointment
and break the other's heart. Better now than
when the damage can no longer be fixed.
> Please don't look at me like that; we both know
> this is not what either of us wanted.

On Being Warded

You sit in a café, your head tilted to one side,
feigning an ear infection you don't have
while your friends commiserate – of course
they understand you can't stay long.
Their laughter is piercing as the clink of spoons
against the walls of coffee cups.
The web of promises you wove to get here
wraps your ankles, like manacles designed
to become tighter the more you struggle.
Among these tables, people move with ease;
swapping chairs and leaning in for a better view
of shared photographs, groups of more than two.
You aren't in any of them. But you nod,
straining against the invisible ropes
that scrape your skin harder
with every *you should've been there*.
In a car just up the street, your bondsman
counts every second with an ice-eyed gaze
that burns through the laughter, and
at the very moment your release expires
you are whisked back to prison
ready or not. Your jailer swings the keys,
satisfied you're still incarcerated.
Confinement has atrophied your muscles
but you are too wild for a cage, so each day after
you push and pull, quietly gathering strength,
and the next time you are briefly paroled,
you slip the rope and run like hell.

Secrets

How heavy is a secret?
a different weight on different shoulders
featherlight on some
on others lead enough
to drown the witch

Double standards
swing like swords
he said, she said
the same things
with very different consequences

He tells the story, safe
in the knowledge his actions
deep in beer and lost control
will be lauded, called heroic--
Theseus to her Ariadne

She wraps the tryst tight, a treasure
concealed from prying eyes
a precious faithlessness
with too high a cost
should she speak

Admission forgives one
and damns the other--
a prison of a different kind
greater love hath no man
than for his reputation

If she tells the same story
with the same words
the brush that gilded him
will stain her with a tar
no years will fade

No Fury

i.
Karma is a bitch and I watched what she did with him that night. My heart ached. I brought you a glass and a bucket to spew bile into and all I could think was *I'm glad it's not me*. You stayed home for six months after that; not even the beach could lure you out.

ii.
Time is elastic like people; both change and stretch. You stretched all the way into another town and I envied you the distance. When you snapped back, you hadn't changed shape at all. But everything around you had rotted and hung loose, like it would slip off your shoulder at any moment. You liked having the space to move.

iii.
A continuum became a circle. Cans of cola morphed into gin martinis and you weren't a spy, but a Bond girl on a vendetta. A stiletto on the sidewalk is as good as one jammed up under the ribcage, right into the heart: worn well, it can have the same effect. Karma might be a bitch but the girl's got style.

iv.
You walked along the water's edge trailing perfume like bait, tweaking the line. He spoke of firsts and lasts while you feigned ignorance as malice burned in your veins. Trap set. He moved towards the open door, but at the last second you slammed it, cutting the line. The tide pulled him out. You let him float away, indifferent.

v.
You learnt how to dodge bullets at a young age, then how to bend time with your fingers. You stretched it, pulled it back on itself. Table turning is a master's trick and you're no apprentice anymore. *I'm glad I'm not you.* I watched what you did to him that night.

Gunpowder Shimmer

Crushed beer cans half buried
in the sand are tiny fractured mirrors
of truth, showing the broken parts of us.
Our hands don't touch. We spent months playing
with matches that failed to spark; you
only light up for an audience
and I'm no pyrotechnician. Here,
where smashed glass is a kaleidoscope
and your colours will be reflected a thousand times
for strangers, you ignite.
In that moment you are magnificent. You bless everyone
with a sprinkling of gold dust and for a moment
everything is Midas-touched, every face
highlighted. Gasps of pleasure, benevolence raining
down—you believe your own hype
and even my lack of faith is shaken.
The explosion, starved of oxygen, extinguishes
as a candle in a bell jar, over as fast
as a falling star without fulfilling any wishes.
Metal-bright in a firework sky…glitter then fade
into a spent cardboard tube, the truth of what you are
when you're not on fire.

In/Visible

stand with one foot in each world—
one above, one below
be nowhere and everywhere
in that space where time stands still
without long exposure
and flows through your fingers
behind the dunes where shadows are longer

moonlight silvers your hair as the sea
a path, an illusion, something
that bridges deeper water
in the small hours

if you leap, will the timbers firm
beneath your feet?

hold the tide's hand, like a stranger
adrift, hopeful, yet knowing
the scars will web like the grain
in driftwood, a small gift,
a talisman worn smooth
an unreadable map

when midnight's spell breaks,
you don't bleed from the clean cut
but wash the wound in earth's womb
and each wave draws back to the ocean,
leaving the sand shiny and new,
unmarked—

Left Overs

The only single girl at a wedding
the size of a state dinner; one dark dress
in a room full of white on white. Push the chicken around
on your plate and wonder whether you could hide it
in the peonies, hide yourself in them. Folks wait
with craned necks for the display of desperation
that comes with the lucky escapee throwing
a token of her bondage at the last condemned
still among her friends. Imagine
standing there, a crowd of one. She pulls you aside,
a whisper of tulle and satin, tells you she knows.
This bride is not a Japanese cine-creature; she's realised
what's about to happen. A light laugh, ribboned roses tossed
on the table and right on through
to the part where the dancing starts.
Bored oldly-weds look around as wedding standards
echo from wooden floors, wondering if
they can get escape from
parental responsibility for just three minutes.
Everyone knows who'll hold the babies, and
we'll all pretend we don't envy each other.

Dealbreakers

He never gave an inkling of what might
be hidden behind the (faux) friendly smiles
the young prince seeks a princess, and finds one--
but the royal family find her lacking

She gives him what he needs – love without the
price tag – no conditions – just her whole heart
no negotiation necessary
at least between him and her…but blood ties

like handcuffs keep him where the queen thinks
he should be, not where he wants. Spinelessness
mutes him; abdication could free them both
the princess sees he will never be king
of his own fate—their hate makes her let him go

his family crown is the black of midnight
and they'll never ever let him wear it

Games People Play

In the field beside the house, with the wrong kind of diamond,
thank God, watching the sun flee from what we both know
is on the other side of night's horizon. The nos far outweigh the yeses.
The game is one-sided and the away team seems destined to win,
even without the home ground advantage.
I leave my face exposed, my clavicles raw,
wait for the sharp blow to the solar plexus--a gut punch or a well-aimed
foul ball. But you can't hit straight. Everything is too tight and you can't
loosen up without a massage. The idea of my hands spreading poison
on your skin repulses us both, and with an electronic buzz
the darkness is banished and so am I.
At home in the darkened lounge, I fall on my mattress in the corner
with my back to every door.
And endlessly in the night, the crack of a baseball bat striking leather
Each light above deep left field shattered, one by one.

Piano Bar, Just After 2am

Slide up, sweet nectar. Candy rim with sugar lips
licked clean. Tart fizz in crystal cylinders
a line of sparkle. Painted fingertips
reach out again, until the ache goes under.
Tiara bent, a diadem askew.
Caricature, decorum gone astray.
She doesn't want to leave, she just wants you
to keep it pretty, make it safe to stay
like this. Beyond the knives. Inadequacy
takes fractured souls. Removes the pieces. She
can't love herself enough. But casually
another swallow. Smile. Rinse and repeat.
A futile patch. A temporary crutch
to make the pain okay, till she wakes up.

It's Not Like That

A ticker tape parade of heart shaped confetti,
rose petals strewn across white linen sheets,
champagne bottles in wet sand,
songs about never ending circles,
and how he'd die for you.

It's not like that.

It's floating in a lake
with your hair around you like mist,
staring at the sky
while the water laps your skin--
holds you up,
supports you,
moulds itself to the curves of your body…
lets you breathe as you rock in the
infinite.

It's knowing as you lay
on the surface of the water
that you can sink

if you want to,
the water will let you--

it will match the tears that leave
your face sparkling,

but never hold on
when you ask it to let you go.

Disassembly

The architecture of separation requires only some Allen keys, time, and determination. Oh, and two large boxes marked *theirs* and *yours*. Strip everything back to its bones; purge the dust, the carnival prizes, the old receipts. Put the photographs in the box marked *theirs* so you don't have to carry the pain of seeing them in the hall cupboard every time you reach for the Christmas lights. Don't worry about labelling the nuts and bolts. They're no longer needed. Remove them one by one, until everything is held together by a single wooden dowel. Hold your breath, knowing it will break but not quite sure when. Watch the shelves crash to the floor under the weight of their own emptiness. Gather the pieces and marvel at how you ever saw beauty in the damage. Put the pieces on the curb for collection. Notice the box marked *yours* is empty. Crush it and add it to the recycling. Leave the box marked *theirs* outside the front door. See the stamp on the side that reads *heavy – requires two people*, and make sure you are gone when the box is collected.

There is Not Enough White in This Room

The edge of my dress is stained with grass and regret while
Dead lilies tumble from your mouth and the vase. There is
Not enough white in this room. The lump in my throat is red and ripe
As Eve's first apple, when she stopped swallowing the truth
And spat it out for all to see, no matter the cost. Action and consequence
Swing against each other as sun and moon,
but only one's light burns.
And even as you convince me of a divine purpose, below the bed
Your feet are aflame.

Le Langage de l'Amour

You can't conjugate French verbs,
so open the champagne and kiss my reflection
like you'd kiss yourself. The mirrorball spins
and I can't dance with you, not that way.
Pour me into glasses, spill me
on the promenade, let my laughter fall
into the water. Say nothing.
Neither of us speaks the language
of love. Your body on mine
is flint against steel
but you and I don't want to start
a fire that needs maintaining.
There are too many sparks.
You stand, with one eyebrow raised,
a lit match between your fingers.
We both know what happens next.
The cobbles tanglefoot my graceful exit, as
over my shoulder the burning bridge
collapses into smoke and ashes.

Aubade With Bus Stop

Do you remember how the sun came in right off the dashboard
on the way to nowhere?
How the clouds hung wispy, illusions of something solid, like candyfloss,
full until you touch it?
You filled the tank, RayBans and surfer cool, while I bought fizzing sherbets
and tried to steal time.
When we got back in the car something slipped through the open door;
it all spilled out, wordless.
I had no idea how to get back from there, so I sat knock-kneed
at the bus stop,
sucking a lemon sweet as you pulled away onto the highway to
wherever you were going.
You didn't spray me with gravel; like the sherbet that exploded in my mouth
you were there, then… gone.
Do you remember what you taught me, that candyfloss day, in the dirt
of a roadside diner?

I want to write about change but the words won't come.

They stick in my throat like promises I know I'll break. There is a waterfall behind the dam of my teeth and I swell to bursting with everything left unsaid. You don't call me anymore; stilted conversation stopped being your style in the winter of '04, when radiator fluid peeled the layer of skin off me that held my tongue. I've come a long way since I stopped keeping those secrets. You still clutch them to your chest in the belief that you can will them into non-existence, consign that part of your life to the void. In the parking lot, I put the Beach Boys on high rotation and bury the last box of heartbreak underneath a dumpster lid. On the road out I watch the jagged skyline recede like worn-down teeth. That town and I have a complicated history; we're like a plastic hula dancer on the dash of a '67 Chevy, both refusing to believe that the best years are behind us.

Self Possession

You seem so self possessed, she says to me; *not self obsessed, that's different. But whenever I see you I'm honestly curious about why you keep sabotaging yourself. It seems like conscious choice. You're so calm, in control. I'm not quite sure what's motivating you...*

I think:
I know exactly what's motivating me, because if I stand in a bar
with a drink in my hand and the right look on my face
the wrong man will come on over and grab me by the hips,
and we'll sway to the music, sticky skin,
and maybe we won't even know each other's names,
and I'll give him my number or not,
and either way I'll know he isn't right
and I won't be disappointed, not even deep down,
and that's how I spare myself the heartache of wanting it to work,
and maybe that song by the Gin Blossoms really is me right now,
and my therapist is sitting there waiting for me to say something,
and I have nothing to say about it aside from it's just what I do,
and if I keep doing it nobody can close enough to hurt me where it counts,
and maybe I'll die young, although God knows I'm not good enough,
and if I say that to her I know she'll take it the wrong way,
and if strong drink and dark alleys haven't killed me yet I must be immortal.

I say:
I'm pretty good at faking, I guess.

Return of Spontaneous Circulation

Not responsive.

I've tried so many times to feel
the rise and fall of ribs,
carotid bounce beneath my
fingertips.

Arrest in progress.

You've stopped. *We've* stopped.
Blue flickers, electrical impulses,
vanished signs of a life
incompatible.

*Not breathing, no pulse,
clinically dead.*

Measure what's left here
in straight lines
and elliptical numbers.

Begin compressions.

Squeeze the life back into it,
replicate the syncopation,
try to make it stay alive.

30:2, compressions to breaths.

Your lips to mine is no rescue.
This is not a golden ratio;
divinity has taken leave.

Check for rhythm.

Fibrillation is an endless plain
devoid of mountains;
monotonous.

Shock required – clear.

Hit it hard, jar it back to
the life expected, before
this lexicon of terminal.

One milligram of adrenaline.

Artificial support, a rush
where there is none;
let's pretend for a moment.

Do we have a ROSC?

Hold your hands,
your breath;
watch the flatline.

It's been too long.

Time of death, 6:34am.

There's no going back.
It's passed.
Stay away from the light.

Acknowledgements

"Piano Bar, Just After 2am" originally appeared in *Chanterelle's Notebook*

"I want to write about change but the words won't come." originally appeared in *The Blue Nib*

About the Author

Amanda McLeod is an Australian author, poet, and artist. She is the author of flash fiction collection *Animal Behaviour* (Chaffinch Press, 2020) and has poetry and fiction published in many places both in print and online. Amanda won the Marjorie Graber-McInnis Short Story Award and the Australian Writers Centre Furious Fiction monthly contest in 2018, and is a Pushcart Prize and Best of the Net nominee. A lover of good coffee and quiet places, she spends as much time outside as she can. Find out more: AmandaMcLeodWrites.com
Twitter and Instagram: @AmandaMWrites

www.ingramcontent.com/pod-product-compliance
Lightning Source LLC
Chambersburg PA
CBHW070043070426
42449CB00012BA/3150